HOW TO OPEN YOUR BANK ACCOUNT IN THE UNITED STATES

Open and Manage Your Business or Personal Account in the USA

VINCENT ALLARD

CorpoMax

Publisher
CorpoMax Publishing LLC

Cover Design
Marie-Andrée Lemieux - malem.com

Cover Image
© nerthuz - 123rf.com

ISBN
E-book ISBN: 978-1-952012-11-2
Paperback ISBN: 978-1-952012-05-1

Edition
First Edition

Series
Third book in the YES TO ENTREPRENEURS® series

CORPOMAX® and YES TO ENTREPRENEURS® are registered trademarks of
CorpoMax Inc. in the United States and other countries, used under license by
CorpoMax Publishing LLC.

WHAT THEY SAY

"Simple. Clear. Precise. Complete. Reading Vincent Allard is having a great time, with a friend who gives us, without pontificating, the best advice to help us succeed in setting up a business in the USA. Cartesian, he divides the challenge into three parts, three books, to properly analyze, explain and better solve difficulties. A must."

Richard JOHNSON, Retired Journalist, Journal of Montreal

"Books such as those in the *Yes to Entrepreneurs* series provide businesses with useful information and practical tools to expand into the United States market, the largest consumer market and recipient of foreign direct investment in the world."

Gina BENTO, Commercial Specialist, U.S. Department of Commerce, International Trade Administration

"Never before have guides been so deserving of the term *practical*! With his trilogy, Vincent Allard offers us in a controlled, organized, complete, but also airy and digestible way everything there is to know about setting up a business in the United States, its name and its banking management. I keep these books on my desk, within easy reach. That is how useful they are."

Bernard GEENEN, Economic and Commercial Counselor, Wallonia Export & Investment Agency, Consulate of Belgium, New York

"I received and read carefully the three guides by Vincent Allard, lawyer and founder of CorpoMax. I am delighted because it is an undeniable help for any entrepreneur who wants to start a business in the United States. It's simple, you are guided and you can feel Vincent Allard's great experience through his advice and recommendations. Also for the legal practitioner, it is a source to many questions that our French and European clients ask us. Congratulations again and thank you!"

Isabelle LANDREAU, Lawyer of the Paris Bar, Founder of Smart Law Fabrik

"My business is advising emerging Canadian companies on developing their business in the United States. I have been doing that for a long time. The aspects of incorporation, setting up bank accounts, even choice of name for doing business in the U.S. can seem complicated. But these guides are great. Everything you need to do is spelled out simply and directly, requirement by requirement, issue by issue. They are ideal for entrepreneurs looking to do business in the United States. Easy to read and to the point. Everything basic that is involved is clearly laid out. I highly recommend their use."

Tom CREARY, Managing Director of WestbridgeOne Consulting, Founder and Past Chairman of the American Chamber of Commerce in Canada - Quebec Chapter

"The *Yes to Entrepreneurs* book series is extremely structured, complete and easy to use, like the services offered by CorpoMax. This solid and valuable work greatly simplifies the task of entrepreneurs, advisers and lawyers. It adds value to our advice and makes the American dream very accessible. We wish this collection a long life and thank Vincent Allard for his permanent dedication."

Serge BOUGANIM, Lawyer of the Paris and Brussels Bars

"Finally a practical and clear guide to answer the questions that any entrepreneur wishing to create a business in the United States is asking !!! The success of an establishment depends above all on good knowledge of the rules of law but also of local commercial practices. In this respect, the corporate name of the company is crucial and the practical advice given by Mr. Allard in his work is particularly relevant and useful. In general, the three books published by Mr. Allard provide a better understanding of the legal issues related to setting up a business in the United States and will help entrepreneurs in carrying out their project."

François BOSCHER, Lawyer of the Tours Bar (1981-1992) and the Quebec Bar (1995- ...), Former President of the French Chamber of Commerce and Industry in Canada - CCIFC

"Congratulations to my colleague Vincent Allard for the publication of three exceptional popularization books for entrepreneurs who want to start a business in the United States. Reference books, advice books, more than 600 pages that guide us in the land of Uncle Sam to get the best results."

Pierre CHAGNON, Retired Emeritus Attorney, Bâtonnier of Quebec

"As someone new to American business, there is so much information, on-line, consultants, advisors, it's all very intimidating. Tell it to me straight... and at last we have it! In easy and amusing terms that gave me confidence in making the right choice, to start my business in America."

Captain Peter FABIAN (ret.), CEO, Advanced Coatings Engineering LLC

"A master at simplifying complex information for all to understand, Vincent Allard has succeeded in putting together a concise, well written and easy to read series on starting a business in the United States. The *Yes to Entrepreneurs* series takes you by the hand and guides you through the steps of incorporating a company, naming it appropriately and even starting a bank account. This series is full of practical information and a must read for both legal professionals looking to gain knowledge in basic American corporate legal issues, and for the motivated entrepreneurs looking to get one step closer to living the American dream."

George VARDATSIKOS, Ph.D.(med.), LL.L., Attorney of the Quebec Bar

"This series of practical guides allows entrepreneurs and professionals who advise them to benefit from the experience of thousands of other entrepreneurs who have started their business in the United States. There are a lot of details that could help their own business."

Robert CHAYER, U.S. Tax Expert, Canada

"Reading highly recommended. Three essential and very comprehensive guides for all immigrant candidates who wish to familiarize themselves with the important concepts to start their professional installation in the United States. These books are very well structured and expose in a very instructive way, but in a simple and accessible language, the concepts to know to make informed decisions concerning their American structure. From the corporate form to the choice of name, including tax implications, everything is there."

Estelle BERENBAUM, Immigration Lawyer, Florida

"Creating companies and doing business in the United States is a journey full of pitfalls. As a European, we underestimate the complexity of American law and its implications. Vincent Allard's Yes to Entrepreneurs collection provides ready-to-use pragmatic knowledge to successfully navigate American *waters*."

Arnaud LABOSSIÈRE, CEO, The Free Minds Press Ltd

"The information contained in Mr. Allard's trilogy of books will be extremely useful to any entrepreneur wishing to enter the U.S. market. The high quality of information is presented in a structured manner and is easily accessible, due to the author's great talent in simplifying complex matters."

Patric BESNER, Besner Business Lawyers

CONTENTS

5 - MERCHANT ACCOUNT AND PAYPAL: YES, IT IS POSSIBLE!

6 - CONCLUSION

EXCLUSIVE BONUS

Throughout the process of writing this guide, I accumulated many hyperlinks that greatly enrich its content.

An up-to-date list of these hyperlinks can be found at the web address listed in the *Useful Resources* section, at the end of this guide.

DEDICATION

I dedicate this practical guide to all foreign entrepreneurs who want to break into the U.S. market but find it difficult to open a bank account. I hope this guide will help them do that.

1 - INTRODUCTION

1.1 - PRESENTATION

Welcome to this practical guide on how to open your bank account in the United States.

My name is Vincent Allard. I am a business lawyer, but first and foremost, an entrepreneur who moved to the United States in 1999. For nearly 20 years, through my website corpomax.com, I have helped thousands of entrepreneurs from more than 50 countries start their businesses in the United States.

OBJECTIVES

This practical guide is mainly intended for you, a foreign entrepreneur who wants to open a business bank account for his or her U.S. company.

It is also for you, a non-U.S. resident who wishes to open a personal bank account in the United States.

This practical guide has two objectives.

Objective no. 1 is to help you understand how the U.S. banking system works, all in simple and clear language.

Objective no. 2 is to provide you with the information you need to open and manage your own bank account in the United States.

ORDER OF PRESENTATION

I strongly recommend that you read this guide from beginning to end, in the order of its presentation. As with a culinary recipe, you need to know the ingredients before baking the cake. Therefore, it is best to follow the exact sequence of this guide and not to skip the steps.

PRACTICAL GUIDE

Attention! This practical guide is not a legal, accounting, or tax guide. For this, you will need to consult professionals working in these areas.

This guide is essentially practical and contains many examples.

In short, this practical guide has been prepared for easy reading and immediate understanding.

I sincerely hope this guide will provide you with the information and inspiration you need to open your bank account in the United States.

If you have any questions, comments, or suggestions regarding this practical guide, including its *Useful Resources* section, please feel free to contact me.

Thank you and good reading!

2 - UNDERSTANDING THE BANKING SYSTEM IN THE UNITED STATES

2.1 - BANKING REGULATION

Unlike many countries that have only one bank regulator, bank operations in the United States are strictly regulated not only by the federal government, but also by the states.

A financial institution doing business in the United States is therefore subject to many federal, state, and sometimes even municipal laws. Indeed, some cities also have their own financial regulation laws.

AREAS

In general, U.S. banking regulations cover seven specific areas:

- Protection of privacy
- Disclosure of banking information
- Prevention of fraud
- Anti-money laundering
- Antiterrorism
- Usury loans
- Promotion of loans to low-income people

2.2 - FEDERAL REGULATORY AGENCIES

Now, let us look at the main banking regulatory agencies in the United States.

FEDERAL RESERVE SYSTEM – FED

Perhaps the most important agency is the Federal Reserve System, often referred to as the Fed. It is the central bank of the United States.

It performs five general functions.

First, the Fed is leading U.S. monetary policy.

Second, it maintains the stability of the financial system in the United States.

Third, it oversees and regulates banking institutions doing business in Uncle Sam's country.

Fourth, it provides financial services to banking institutions and the U.S. federal government.

Finally, it promotes American consumer protection as well as community development.

FEDERAL DEPOSIT INSURANCE CORPORATION - FDIC

A second federal regulatory agency is the Federal Deposit Insurance Corporation (FDIC).

The FDIC is a governmental corporation that performs four main functions.

First, the FDIC offers deposit insurance, which guarantees the security of deposits in more than 6,000 banks in the United States. The guarantee is up to $250,000 per depositor per bank.

Second, it reviews and supervises the security and soundness of the banks.

Third, it performs certain functions related to consumer protection.

Finally, it manages banks in difficulty or in bankruptcy, which it takes care of and temporarily administers. Generally, these problematic banks are then sold or merged with existing banks.

The FDIC maintains a list of troubled banks on its website.

Since the launch of the FDIC in 1934, there has been no loss of insured funds following the bankruptcy of a bank.

OFFICE OF THE COMPTROLLER OF THE CURRENCY - OCC

Another federal regulatory agency is the Office of the Comptroller of the Currency (OCC).

This U.S. federal agency has several functions, the main ones being as follows.

First, the OCC licenses, regulates, and supervises U.S. domestic banks and foreign bank agencies operating in the United States.

Second, it ensures the soundness and security of the American banking system.

Third, it promotes competition by allowing banks to offer new products and services.

Fourth, it ensures fair and equal access to financial services for all Americans.

Fifth, it applies the laws concerning the fight against money laundering and terrorist financing.

Finally, it investigates cases of misconduct on the part of:

- Institutions affiliated with national banks
- Directors, officers, and employees of banks
- Independent agents and contractors working in the banking sector
- Professionals working in the banking sector, such as lawyers, accountants, tax experts, appraisers, etc.

OFFICE OF THRIFT SUPERVISION - OTS

Another federal regulatory agency is the Office of Thrift Supervision (OTS). Established in 1989, this U.S. federal agency reports to the Treasury Department and is part of the Office of the Comptroller of the Currency. It is the first federal regulator for federal and state financial institutions dedicated to savings.

It has three main functions.

First, the OTS licenses savings banks.

Second, it supervises the savings banks.

Finally, it adopts and applies the regulations to savings banks.

OFFICE OF FOREIGN ASSETS CONTROL - OFAC

Another federal regulatory agency is the Office of Foreign Assets Control (OFAC). It is a financial intelligence and law enforcement agency. Reporting to the U.S. Treasury Department, this agency is probably the most powerful and least known of U.S. federal agencies.

Its main functions include the following.

First, the OFAC operates against foreign countries, individuals, and organisations, using enormous powers conferred on it by law.

Second, it administers and enforces the embargoes imposed by the United States. For example, it is the OFAC that has been enforcing the economic, commercial, and financial embargo against Cuba since 1962.

Third, it administers and enforces economic and trade sanctions imposed by the United States in at least three ways:

- It imposes very significant fines. For example, in 2014, the OFAC imposed a fine of nearly $1 billion on the French bank BNP Paribas.
- It orders freezes of assets. For example, the OFAC regularly decrees the freezing of assets belonging to terrorist groups or countries promoting terrorism.
- It issues prohibitions to operate in the United States. For example, the OFAC prohibits any Iranian company from doing business on U.S. soil.

Finally, it publishes at least two lists:

- The first list is the *Specially Designated Nationals And Blocked Persons List* (SDN). This is a list of people, organizations, aircraft, and ships with whom American citizens and companies cannot do business.
- The second list is the *Sectoral Sanctions Identifications List* (SSI). This is a list of people, companies, and entities in the sectors of the Russian economy with whom it is prohibited to do business in the United States. Particularly targeted sectors are energy, finance, and armaments.

2.3 - ANTI-MONEY LAUNDERING AND ANTITERRORISM

In order to fight money laundering and terrorism, the United States has adopted several financial transparency rules, forcing U.S. banks to implement control measures.

These rules impose three main obligations on banks:

- First, they must know their customers.
- Second, they must understand their customers' current and predictable transactions.
- Finally, they must keep records and report on their customers.

In this sense, a series of laws have been adopted by the United States.

BANK SECRECY ACT - BSA

Among the most important is the Bank Secrecy Act (BSA).

This law is also often referred to as AML, for Anti-Money Laundering Law, or as the combined acronym BSA-AML.

Adopted in 1970, this law forces financial institutions in the United States to fulfill three main obligations.

The first obligation is to assist U.S. government agencies in detecting and preventing money laundering.

The second obligation is to keep records of all purchases of negotiable instruments in cash. An example of a negotiable instrument is a bank check or a traveler's check.

The third obligation is to file several reports.

- The first report is the Currency Transaction Report (CTR). This report must indicate any transaction or series of transactions totaling more than $10,000 in cash in a single day.
- The second report is the Suspicious Activity Report (SAR). This report must mention any suspicious activity that may be related to money laundering, tax evasion, or any other criminal activity. It should be noted that financial institutions have absolutely no right to inform their customers that a report has been filed about them.
- Finally, the third report is the Monetary Instrument Log (MIL). This report must mention any cash purchase of monetary instruments, such as money orders, bank checks, or traveler's checks, ranging in size from $3,000 to $10,000.

If banks fail to adequately fulfill all or part of these three obligations, the law provides for very significant penalties and sometimes even prison.

USA PATRIOT ACT

The second law of importance is the USA Patriot Act.

In the United States, we really like acronyms. Did you know that *USA Patriot Act* actually is actually the acronym for *Uniting and Strength-*

ening America by Providing Appropriate Tools Required to Intercept and Obstruct Terrorism Act of 2001?

Adopted at speed on October 26, 2001, about 45 days after the sad events of September 11, this law includes a comprehensive chapter on measures to be taken against money laundering.

The USA Patriot Act aims to facilitate the prevention, detection, and suppression of money laundering and terrorist financing. This steel-toothed law includes three sections that have the following objectives:

- The first objective is to strengthen banking rules against money laundering, especially on the international scene.
- The second objective is to improve communication between law enforcement agencies and financial institutions, and to expand record-keeping and reporting requirements.
- The third objective is to prevent the smuggling and counterfeiting of money by, among other things, quadrupling the maximum penalty for counterfeiting foreign currency.

The USA Patriot Act is a law with temporary effects, but regularly renewed, often with changes dictated by the political mood of the moment.

2.4 - TYPES OF BANKS

In the United States, there are four main types of banks.

NATIONAL BANKS

First of all, there are national banks.

These banks are formed and regulated by the Office of the Comptroller of the Currency (OCC).

The name of the bank must contain the word *National*, the designation *National Association,* or the acronym *N.A.* Generally, you will not see any of these legal identifiers on the bank's outside banner or logo. It is rather in the legal documents that you will find the legal identifier, for example in the contract that you will sign with the bank.

Here are some examples of national banks:

- Bank of America
- Chase
- Citibank
- Wells Fargo

The advantage of having a charter under the *National Bank Act* is that the bank is not subject to state laws on predatory lending. There is no cap on the interest rates charged by national banks. The only requirement is to disclose to consumers the nature and extent of fees, interest rates, and terms.

Finally, despite their name, some national banks are limited to a single state, county, or city.

FEDERAL SAVINGS BANKS

As a second type of bank, there are the federal savings banks. They are also known as federal savings associations.

These banks are created and regulated by the Office of Thrift Supervision (OTS).

The name of the bank must contain the word *Federal* or the initials *F.S.B.*

Here are some examples of federal savings banks:

- First Federal Savings Bank
- Lincoln Federal Savings Bank
- Security Federal Savings Bank
- Time Federal Savings Bank

CREDIT UNIONS

As a third type of bank, there are credit unions.

These financial institutions are not-for-profit organizations. As a result, they are not subject to any tax at the federal or state level.

Credit unions are generally created for a defined segment of the population, such as:

- Company employees
- Church members
- Union members

Here are some examples of credit unions:

- California Credit Union
- Credit Union West
- United Local Credit Union

The largest credit union in the United States is the Navy Federal Credit Union. It serves employees and contractors of the Department of Defense, as well as their families.

Credit unions can be created in two ways:

1. By the federal government

In such a case, they are called *federal credit unions.*

2. By a state

All but three U.S. states can create credit unions. In Delaware, South Dakota, and Wyoming, where there is no such bank legislation, only federal credit unions can do business there.

Under the jurisdiction of the National Credit Union Administration — NCUA, credit unions are very popular in the United States. They serve over 100 million members, or nearly 45% of the U.S. labor force.

Deposits of credit union members are insured up to $250,000 by the National Credit Union Share Insurance Fund — NCUSIF —, an organization supported by the U.S. federal government. However, this program is administered by the National Credit Union Administration — NCUA.

STATE BANKS

Finally, as a fourth type of bank, there are state banks.

These banks are incorporated and regulated by the states. Therefore, they cannot have the words *National* or *Federal* in their name.

Here are some examples of state banks:

- Farmers State Bank
- Northern State Bank of Virginia
- State Bank of Southern Utah
- Tennessee State Bank

If the state bank is a member of the Federal Reserve, commonly known as the Fed, it is also regulated by it.

If it is not a member, it is regulated by the FDIC.

In other words, each state bank is subject to at least two regulatory bodies:

- Federal agency - Fed or FDIC
- State agency

Generally, state banks are purely local community banks, and sometimes have only one branch.

2.5 - ACTIVE BANKS IN THE UNITED STATES

To give you a brief overview of the American banking system, let us look at some statistics.

In the United States, there are nearly 5,000 active commercial banks. There are more than 700 savings banks in operation.

Despite these impressive figures, there are fewer than 100 problem banks.

LARGE BANKS

Major American banks include:

- Bank of America
- Citibank
- JP Morgan Chase
- US Bank
- Wells Fargo

The FDIC website is full of data and statistics about banks in the United States.

3 - ALL ABOUT BANK ACCOUNTS IN THE UNITED STATES

3.1 - TYPES OF BANK ACCOUNTS

In the United States, there are basically two types of bank accounts.

For a company, there is the business account.

For an individual, there is the personal account.

A personal account can be simple, with only one signatory, or joint, with two or more signatories. In the latter case, it is called a joint account.

~

Both in the case of a business account and a personal account, there are the same variations. In both cases, you can get one of the following accounts:

CHECKING ACCOUNT

The first and probably the most popular type of account is a checking account.

This type of account earns little or no interest. It offers basic services only. For example, it is usually necessary to pay to obtain a checkbook.

Additional fees are charged if there is a lot of activity in the account. For example, a fee may be charged if more than ten checks are processed on a monthly basis.

A variation of the checking account, called *interest-bearing checking account*, offers interest that varies according to the balance of the account. Account maintenance fees are higher. However, the account holder can generally issue an unlimited number of checks.

Remember that banks offer several types of checking accounts, each with its own pros and cons.

SAVINGS ACCOUNT

The second type of account is a savings account.

It allows you to make deposits and withdrawals, but you cannot issue checks. The interest provided by this type of account is higher than that offered by a checking account.

MONEY MARKET ACCOUNT

The third type of account is a money market account.

The money deposited in this account is invested by the bank in low-risk investments. The interest earned on this account is higher than that earned on a checking or savings account. Moreover, the interest rate increases when the account balance increases.

CERTIFICATE OF DEPOSIT

Finally, the last type of account is a certificate of deposit.

The amount of money deposited in this account is frozen for a specified period of time, often ranging from three months to six years. The interest rate on this type of account is higher. And precisely because of the freezing of the amount invested, the longer the term, the higher the interest rate. Finally, there is a significant penalty if there is an early withdrawal of the amount invested in this account.

FDIC

Note that all these accounts are insured by the FDIC up to a maximum of $250,000 per depositor per financial institution.

MULTI-CURRENCY ACCOUNT

Several U.S. banks also offer the possibility of having a multi-currency account, also referred to as a foreign currency account.

However, some banks require that holders of a multi-currency account have U.S. citizenship or be U.S. residents. Also, the monthly fees charged by banks for a multi-currency account are generally quite high.

One of the few banks that systematically offer multi-currency accounts is the international bank HSBC. However, with this bank, you cannot normally open an account for your American company if it does not have a real physical place of business in the United States.

FOREIGN BANK ACCOUNT IN U.S. CURRENCY

There is a big difference between a U.S. bank account and a foreign bank account in U.S. currency. The U.S. banking clearing system is different from foreign banking clearing systems.

For example, a Canadian check issued in U.S. dollars is treated in the United States as a foreign check, with the additional costs and delays involved.

.   .   .

This is why it is always better to open a U.S. bank account for your U.S. company, not a U.S. currency bank account in your country of residence.

3.2 - BANK DOCUMENTS TO SIGN

Before your business or personal account is opened in the United States, you must sign several bank documents.

CONTRACT WITH THE BANK

The first document is the contract with the bank. It is designated in various ways:

- Account Agreement
- Account Bank Agreement
- Bank Account Agreement
- Bank Agreement
- Bank Deposit Agreement
- Bank Services Agreement
- Banking Service Agreement
- Deposit Account Agreement
- Service Agreement

In addition to being very long, written in legal terms difficult to understand, and printed in small characters, this contract is non-negotiable. So in real life, nobody reads it.

Among its many provisions, the contract provides that, like you, the bank may close the account without notice or reason provided.

SIGNATURE CARD

The second document is the signature card.

For a business account, all authorized signatories must sign.

For a personal account, the individual must sign. For a joint personal account, all individuals must sign.

This signature card simply allows the bank to compare signatures with those that will be affixed to future bank documents, such as checks.

BANK RESOLUTION

In the case of a business account, the third document is the bank resolution.

It is a legal document of a corporate nature, which specifically authorizes one or more individuals to sign for and on behalf of the company.

Generally, the authorized signatories of a U.S. company are one or more of its directors or officers - President, Vice President, Secretary, Treasurer, CEO, etc.

BENEFICIAL OWNER FORM

Finally, still for a business account, the last document to sign is a beneficial owner form.

In this form, authorized signatories must answer a series of questions to determine the true identity of the beneficial owners of the bank account. Remember the disclosure requirements imposed on banks by various laws, including the *Bank Secrecy Act* and the *USA Patriot Act*.

SIGNING OF FORMS

The signature of all these banking documents by the customer is usually affixed to a tablet-style electronic terminal, directly in front of the banker. This is a way for the bank compliance department to ensure that the customer is actually present at the branch when signing. As a result, the signing of paper bank forms is becoming increasingly rare.

In addition, the customer's signature must be affixed to the line provided for this purpose. In Europe, it seems that the location of the signature does not really matter, as long as it is affixed somewhere on the document. In the United States, the signature must be affixed on the line provided for this purpose. Otherwise, the document is presumed unsigned.

3.3 - BANK ACCOUNT DETAILS

ROUTING NUMBER

The first number of the contact details of a U.S. bank account is the routing number.

Even though the popular expression in the United States is *routing number*, this number has several names:

- ABA routing transit number
- ABA routing number
- ABA number
- ABA RTN
- Routing transit number

The routing number is a nine-digit number. It is always indicated at the bottom of a check, usually on the left. This number is based on the geographical location of the bank or branch in which the account was opened. This is a public number that can easily be found on the Internet.

ACCOUNT NUMBER

The second number is the account number. This is the number of the personal or business bank account opened in the name of the individual or company.

It is generally a number from nine to thirteen digits. This second sequence of numbers appears at the bottom of the check, usually to the right of the routing number.

BIC CODE OR SWIFT CODE

The third number is the BIC code or SWIFT code. The acronym *BIC* stands for *Bank Identifier Code*. The word *SWIFT* is actually the acronym for *Society for Worldwide Interbank Financial Telecommunications*.

In everyday reality, this code is called in various ways:

- BIC code
- SWIFT-BIC
- SWIFT code
- SWIFT ID

This is a unique identification code for financial institutions. Usually composed of eight or eleven alphanumeric characters - a combination of letters and numbers - this code is used to transfer money between banks, especially for international bank transfers.

RIB AND IBAN

In France, when you need to provide your bank account information to someone, you can provide either of the following numbers:

- Your RIB - *Relevé d'Identité Bancaire* or bank details - for domestic use OR

- Your IBAN - *International Bank Account Number* - for international use

However, the notions of RIB and IBAN do not exist in the United States. These are purely European concepts.

IN BRIEF

So, to fully identify a U.S. bank account, you need:

- Two numbers for domestic use — routing number and account number
- Three numbers for international use — routing number, account number, and BIC-SWIFT code.

3.4 - BANK ACCOUNT MANAGEMENT

There are two main ways to manage your U.S. bank account.

IN-BRANCH MANAGEMENT

The first way to manage your bank account is at a branch. However, keep in mind the following. Even if your account has been opened in a certain branch, nothing attaches you to that branch. In other words, you can manage your account from any branch of the bank, regardless of the state in which it is located. For example, your account was opened at a Bank of America branch in New York City. Afterwards, you can manage it very well by going to a branch in Miami, Las Vegas, or San Francisco.

In fact, do not expect to establish a rewarding relationship with an American banker. There is a high turnover rate of bank staff in the United States, especially in large banks located in major cities.

Actually, there is no real advisor assigned to your account. And when there is one, chances are they will already be replaced when you need to contact them.

MANAGEMENT VIA THE INTERNET

The second way to manage your bank account is via the Internet. A computer, tablet, or mobile phone makes it easy for you to perform day-to-day banking transactions.

You must create your access to the online account. In this sense, you usually need your bank card, PIN, and account number. Often, the banking interface will ask you to provide your SSN, which is the U.S. social security number. However, for those who are not U.S. citizens or residents, there is often a hyperlink that indicates *I do not have a SSN*. In such a case, there are some additional questions you will need to answer. You may also need to contact the bank customer service department. Finally, in rare cases, it is possible to replace the SSN with a series of nine zeros.

SECURITY

Of course, the bank insists on security to prevent third parties from illegally accessing your account. In this sense, you will need to provide an answer to some security questions that may be asked when you try to access your account over the Internet. If you can choose the questions yourself, make sure they are not too simple or too easy to answer. Some increase the level of security by providing answers unrelated to the questions.

TWO-STEP VERIFICATION

Another effective security measure is the two-step verification system, known as *Two-Step Verification* or *Two-Factor Authentication*. This security measure allows you to receive on your mobile phone - by SMS or through an authentication application - a six-digit code that must be indicated on the interface to access your online bank account, at least the first time.

But to do this, you need one of the following:

- A U.S. mobile phone
- A mobile phone with a U.S. or international SIM card
- A U.S. virtual phone number that allows you to receive SMS or text messages.

3.5 - BANK CARDS

There are several types of bank cards in the United States.

ATM CARD

The first type of bank card is an ATM card.

A cash distributor is called an ATM for *automated teller machine.*

The ATM card is directly linked to your bank account. When you use it, there is an immediate debit in your account. If there is not enough money available, the card cannot make the desired transaction, unless your account has protection against any overdraft.

The ATM card operates with a personal identification number - PIN. The PIN consists of at least four digits.

The advantage of such a card is important. In case of loss or theft, whoever finds your card cannot use it without the PIN.

But there are also some disadvantages. First, there is often a small annual fee associated with the ATM card. Second, this card cannot generally be used to make purchases via the Internet. Finally, this card is only used to make cash withdrawals from the ATM or to perform other basic banking operations, such as depositing checks, paying bills, and obtaining information on the account balance.

DEBIT CARD

The second type of bank card is a debit card, sometimes called a check card.

It is a hybrid solution that combines the ATM card and the credit card.

In short, this card is the equivalent of a credit card with immediate debit. It looks exactly like a real credit card. However, it usually includes the words *Debit Card* or simply *Debit* on its front.

The debit card also has a digital sequence identical to that of a regular credit card, in addition to displaying the Visa or MasterCard logo.

This card generally does not charge any issuance or annual fees. Sometimes, it even provides points for making purchases.

Finally, the use of this card may be subject to a daily limit, both for withdrawals at the ATM and for purchases. However, this limit can easily be increased upon request.

CREDIT CARD

The third type of bank card is a credit card.

The credit card is not linked to your bank account. So, there is no immediate debit. But its balance is payable once a month.

The great advantage of this card is that you are generally not responsible for purchases made by a third party in case of loss, theft, or fraudulent use. Therefore, it offers better protection against fraud than other types of cards.

. . .

However, there are two main disadvantages.

First, the credit card imposes a monthly purchase limit, unlike the ATM card or debit card.

Second, in case of non-payment or insufficient payment of the balance by the due date, interest, penalties, and late fees are automatically charged.

Finally, note that the chances of obtaining a credit card in the United States are very low if you are not a U.S. citizen or resident, with a Social Security Number - SSN.

～

The bank card we are mainly going to talk about is the debit card, which is the one issued by the bank when opening your account. We will simply call it the card or bank card.

～

ON YOUR BANK CARD

So, what is on your bank card, in addition to its number and expiration date?

When associated with a personal account, your card has only your name on it. In the United States, the first name always precedes the last name.

When associated with a business account, your card includes your name and that of your company. There is no bank card issued only in the company's name. Indeed, this would be problematic in case of loss or theft.

ISSUING YOUR BANK CARD

As a general rule, the banker requires your bank card to be issued as soon as the account is opened. Nevertheless, it is still recommended to check with the banker to ensure that your card will be issued.

The card will be mailed to your U.S. address approximately five to seven business days after opening the account. If you request that it be mailed outside the United States, you will be at significant risk because of loss issues that may arise from international mail delivery.

TEMPORARY BANK CARD

Some banks offer the possibility of obtaining a temporary bank card, upon request, when opening your account.

When meeting with the banker, do not hesitate to request this temporary card and its PIN. This will allow you to immediately create your Internet access, so you do not have to wait to receive the official card and its PIN by mail.

ACTIVATING YOUR BANK CARD

The method of activating your card varies from one bank to another. But, in general, there are four methods of activation:

- ATM
- Bank app on your mobile device
- Bank website
- Telephone

USING YOUR BANK CARD

Now, a few words about using your bank card.

If you use your card in an ATM and you make the mistake of entering a wrong PIN three times, the ATM simply swallows your card.

In addition, if you make cash withdrawals from your company's business account to the ATM on a regular basis, this may prompt the bank compliance department to close this account without notice.

In the United States, it is unusual to make cash withdrawals from a business account.

Indeed, a company normally makes withdrawals in three ways:

- By check
- By payment with a bank card
- By transfer

Of course, if you withdraw a small amount of cash on an irregular basis, this should not be a problem.

But, if you withdraw a large amount of cash on a regular basis, it will attract the attention of the bank compliance department, whose mission includes detecting money laundering.

ONE-TIME CARD NUMBERS

In the United States, it is possible to create card numbers for one-time use. Some banks and websites allow you to create a single-use card number for a specific amount. Once this number is used, it is no longer available for other transactions.

MOBILE PAYMENT APPLICATIONS

Another way to protect your card number is to use any of the Apple Pay, Samsung Pay, Google Pay or similar services on your mobile phone. Their technology ensures that a completely different card number is generated and communicated to the merchant during every purchase transaction, in an encrypted way.

USING YOUR CARD OUTSIDE THE UNITED STATES

If you plan to use your card outside the United States, it is suggested to notify the bank, so that it does not block its use. Often, the bank's website or mobile application allows you to specify the dates on which your bank card will be used outside the United States.

PROBLEMS WITH YOUR BANK CARD

If your bank card is stolen, lost, or used fraudulently, you must immediately contact the bank. In fact, you should keep the bank's phone number, indicated on the back of the card, in your mobile phone contacts.

Generally, the bank's mobile application allows you to immediately block the use of your card.

If your card is broken, you must notify the bank without delay. In the United States, it took many years for chips to appear on bank cards. Despite this, many cards still have a magnetic strip on the back, which invariably degrades and stops working.

Finally, if your card is blocked in an ATM, after three unsuccessful attempts, you must contact the bank to report the situation and ask for a replacement. This request can also be made on the bank's website or by using the mobile application.

INTERPRETER SERVICES

In any case, if you are not fluent in English, simply ask the bank representative to provide you with an interpreter in your native language - free of charge. For example, from the beginning of the conversation, all you have to say is: *I need a Spanish interpreter*. Normally, in less than five minutes, the interpreter will join the conversation. This interpreter service, unfortunately not well known, is usually provided by major U.S. banks.

3.6 - BANK STATEMENTS

On a monthly basis, the bank will send you an account statement.

ANALYSIS OF YOUR BANK STATEMENT

The bank account statement includes the following information:

- Account number
- Bank fees
- Cashed checks
- Period covered
- Points earned
- Transaction history

For the period covered, it often extends from the first to the last day of the month. Sometimes, the period covered begins when the account is opened and ends 30 or 31 days later. It all depends on the bank. However, it is possible to ask your bank to change the period covered by the statement, if it is more convenient for you.

I suggest you always carefully analyze the details of bank charges. Never make the mistake of believing that the bank never does.

PAPERLESS BANK STATEMENTS

Finally, it is better to opt for virtual account statements - paperless - rather than printed ones.

The advantages of this solution are numerous:

Ecological

First, it is an ecological solution. Collectively, let's save some trees.

Convenient

Second, it is a practical solution. Your account statements are easily accessible, in PDF format, on the bank's website. You can download and save them in a folder on your computer, tablet, or mobile phone. This makes it much easier to view and archive them.

Economic

Third, it is an economical solution. You have no shipping costs to pay. In fact, some banks now charge a monthly fee of $2 to $5 to send you a printed statement.

Fast

Fourth, it is a quick solution. As soon as your account statement is issued, you will immediately receive an email.

Confidential

Finally, this is a solution that ensures the confidentiality of your financial affairs. This prevents the possible loss of your account statements in the dungeons of the U.S. or foreign postal system. Even better, it prevents your statements from falling into the wrong hands.

3.7 - BANK CHECKS

There are various types of checks in the United States.

BANK CHECK

First of all, there is a bank check. This is simply the check issued by the bank account holder.

CASHIER'S CHECK

Then there is a cashier's check. This is an official check issued by the financial institution where the holder's account is located.

MONEY ORDER

Then there is a money order. This is a check issued by a bank, a post office, a grocery store, or a gas station. The amount of this money order is generally limited to $1,000. The cost of issuing the money order is usually higher at the banks than at the post office.

TRAVELER'S CHECK

Finally, there is a traveler's check. This type of check was popularized as early as 1891 by the American Express credit card issuer. However, traveler's checks are much less popular today, partly because of the global use of credit and debit cards.

∽

ANALYSIS OF A BANK CHECK

Now, let us take a closer look at what is included in a bank check, that is, the check issued by the account holder.

First, at the top left of the check, is the name of the account holder. Some U.S. organizations will refuse your check if it does not include your name or that of your company.

Under the name, there is usually the address of the check issuer. Often, there is also his or her phone number. Again, some U.S. agencies may refuse your check if it does not include your address and phone number. Therefore, when ordering a checkbook from a U.S. bank, be sure to ask for your name, address, and phone number to appear on it.

Then, of course, we find the name of the bank.

At the top right, the date must be affixed. Here are some ways used in the United States to indicate the date on a check:

- September 1, 2020
- Sept 1, 2020
- 9-1-2020
- 9-1-20
- 2020-09-01

Then, the amount of the check is indicated, in words and figures.

Below is the name of the beneficiary.

The beneficiary's address is not mandatory. The address appears especially when companies or government agencies send checks printed mechanically. The name and address of the check beneficiary therefore appear in the transparent plastic part of the envelope.

At the bottom of the check, we find some numbers. The sequence of numbers often begins with the routing number. Then, the account number of the check issuer is indicated. As for the check number - usually indicated at the top right - it also appears in an encoded way at the bottom of the check. Depending on the banks, this encoded number appears either before the routing number or after the account number.

ENDORSEMENT OF A CHECK

In the United States, it is mandatory that a check be endorsed before being deposited in your bank account. In the branch, if you fail to endorse the check, the bank clerk will ask you to do so. But if you deposit an unendorsed check in an ATM - Automated Teller Machine - the check will be returned by the bank, uncleared, for lack of endorsement.

TYPES OF ENDORSEMENTS

In the United States, there are three ways to endorse a check.

Blank Endorsement

First, there is the blank endorsement. The check beneficiary simply signs the back of the check. It is recommended to endorse a check only when you are at the bank counter to deposit the check in your account, or when you deposit the check in an ATM. Indeed, as soon as you endorse a check, it becomes payable to the bearer, which can be problematic in case of loss or theft.

. . .

Restrictive Endorsement

Second, there is the restrictive endorsement. An endorsement is restrictive when the mention *For Deposit Only* or *For Deposit Only to Account No. 1234* appears on the back of the check, in addition to your signature. In this case, the check must be deposited in the beneficiary bank account. Moreover, it is always better to endorse a check restrictively than to endorse it in blank.

Special Endorsement

Finally, there is the special endorsement. In this case, the beneficiary endorses the check in favor of another person, adding the words *Pay to the Order of Paul Smith*, followed by his or her signature. This type of endorsement is only possible if the check is issued to an individual and not to a company.

LIFETIME OF A CHECK

The life of a check is usually six months. Indeed, under U.S. laws, banks are not legally required to honor a check that is dated more than six months. Nothing prevents them from doing so, but it is quite rare.

POST-DATED CHECK

In addition, the notion of post-dated checks does not exist in the United States. For example, on March 1st, you issue a check dated June 1st. Nothing prevents the beneficiary from depositing this check as of March 1st. As a general rule, the bank will honor this check, even if its date is later than the date of its deposit.

CHECK DEPOSIT BY SCAN

Today, it is possible to deposit a check without physically going to the bank. Indeed, technology allows checks to be deposited through a scanner or a mobile application. This is very convenient for everyone, including people residing outside the United States who want to deposit a check into their U.S. bank account.

CHECK ISSUED IN FOREIGN CURRENCY

Depositing a check issued in foreign currency in a U.S. bank is sometimes laborious.

First of all, it is often necessary to forward this foreign check to a particular department of the bank. In fact, U.S. bank branches are often poorly equipped to process foreign checks.

Second, the time it takes to cash foreign checks can sometimes take up to six months.

Finally, bank fees associated with cashing a foreign check are often exorbitant. For example, in some banks, cashing a foreign check costs $75, regardless of its amount. However, in other banks, the fee for cashing the same check is only $5.

3.8 - BANK TRANSFERS

There are different ways to make a transfer from your U.S. bank account.

BANK BRANCH

The first and probably the least convenient way is to go to one of your bank's branches.

Each bank is different and therefore has its own requirements. In some cases, the bank will require your physical presence, in front of a banker, to make a transfer.

INTERNET

The second way to make a transfer is through the bank's website, in your customer area, or via the bank's application on your mobile phone.

However, there is often a limit — daily, weekly, or monthly — to the amount you can transfer. In order to get around this limit, the bank can provide you, on request, with a security token which costs about $20.

This authentication token randomly generates a code, thereby increasing the limit on authorized bank transfers.

EMAIL OR FAX

In the United States, it is generally no longer possible to request a bank transfer by email or fax.

Indeed, especially since September 11, 2001, security measures have been drastically increased, particularly at the banking level. Moreover, it significantly reduces the cases of identity theft.

SSN AND ITIN

On rare occasions, some banks will require you to have a U.S. Social Security Number - SSN - or a U.S. Non-Resident Tax ID - ITIN - before allowing you to make a bank transfer.

ALTERNATIVE SOLUTIONS

To avoid this type of restriction and especially to reduce bank charges, some websites, including TransferWise, offer an alternative solution. They allow you to link your bank accounts anywhere in the world and make transfers between them or to other bank accounts, at a much more reasonable price.

3.9 - BANK FEES

The list of fees your U.S. bank charges you is not always easy to find. It is often hidden on the bank's website. However, it is important to compare the fees charged by your bank with those of another bank.

LIST OF BANK FEES

There are often two versions of the list of bank fees.

First, there is a detailed version, which sometimes accompanies bank statements or is available on the bank's website in PDF format.

There is also a simplified version, available on the bank's website, which gives an overview of the main fees, in a way that is much easier to read and understand.

Now, let us take a look at the main bank fees.

ACCOUNT MAINTENANCE FEES

Bank charges include account maintenance fees, which are billed on a monthly basis. These fees normally range from $5 to $30 per month, depending on the type of account. There are often ways to avoid paying these fees if you keep a minimum balance in your account.

Some banks or account types will require you to maintain a fixed minimum balance. For example, your account must maintain a minimum balance of $2,000 at any time during the month.

Other banks or account types will instead require you to maintain an average minimum balance. For example, your account must have an average minimum balance of $2,000 during the month. This means that the account may have a balance of less than $2,000 at any one time during the month and a balance greater than $2,000 at another time in the month. What is important is that the average minimum balance, calculated at the end of the month, be at least $2,000.

Finally, other banks or account types will require you to use your bank card a minimum number of times during the month, or to make one or more deposits or withdrawals during the same period.

BANK CARD FEES

Regarding the card issued by the bank when opening your account, there are generally no fees for issuing this card. However, if it is an ATM card, a fee of about $10 per year is often charged.

There is usually no monthly fee for using your bank card to make purchases or withdrawals at any of the bank's ATMs. However, there are generally fees if you make withdrawals from an ATM other than your bank's. Finally, if your card is used outside the United States, the fees associated with each transaction are often quite high.

BANK DEPOSIT FEES

Bank deposit fees vary from bank to bank. In general, there is no fee for depositing U.S. checks, unless the total checks deposited during the month exceeds a certain limit. However, there may be fees when you deposit foreign checks issued in U.S. dollars, or foreign checks issued in foreign currency.

Also, there may be charges when you deposit cash into your account. Again, it all depends on the type of bank account, the benefits attached to it, and the limits on the number of cash deposits or the total amount of such deposits.

BANK TRANSFER FEES

Fees for domestic bank transfers, that is, between two U.S. accounts, are relatively small.

On the other hand, fees related to international bank transfers are quite high.

First, there are the visible costs. These are the ones that the bank requires you to make a transfer. For example, a fee of $40 is charged if the banker prepares the transfer for you, or $25 if you prepare the transfer yourself on the bank's website or mobile application.

There are also, and above all, invisible costs. These are the ones that are hidden in the currency conversion rate.

But fortunately, as we have seen previously, there are now much cheaper solutions when you want to transfer money from your U.S. bank account to a foreign one. Indeed, more and more websites offer transfer services at a reasonable price, with no hidden fees in the currency conversion rate.

3.10 - BANK CUSTOMER SERVICE

In the United States, customer service varies greatly from one bank to another. There is no single way to meet the expectations of banking customers. Some banks have understood this perfectly. But we can still analyze the main ways to contact your bank for information or assistance.

1. TELEPHONE SERVICE

The first way to contact the bank is by phone. As a general rule, each major bank offers telephone service seven days a week, 24 hours a day, for any problem with your Internet access or bank card. This service is offered for any type of account, both business and personal. For any other matter relating to your business account, bank representatives are normally available Monday to Friday, during normal business hours.

NORMAL BUSINESS HOURS

The concept of normal business hours varies by bank and by region.

In the United States, time is based on a cycle of 12 hours, not 24. This means that:

- 9 o'clock in the morning is written as *9 a.m.* - from the Latin *ante meridiem* or before noon.
- 9 o'clock in the evening is written *9 p.m.* - from the Latin *post meridiem* or after noon.

For example, we say that a bank is open *from 9 a.m. to 5 p.m.*, and not *from 9 to 17*.

Furthermore, the United States has 11 time zones. The most common are:

- Eastern Standard Time (e.g., New York)
- Central Standard Time (e.g., Chicago)
- Pacific Standard Time (e.g., Los Angeles)

In order to define the time in a particular location, we say:

- *From 9 to 5 EST*: from 9 a.m. to 5 p.m., Eastern Standard Time
- *From 9 to 5 CST*: from 9 a.m. to 5 p.m., Central Standard Time
- *From 9 to 5 PST*: from 9 a.m. to 5 p.m., Pacific Standard Time

For example, there is a three-hour time difference between the city of Los Angeles - Pacific Standard Time - and New York City - Eastern Standard Time.

In addition, the time varies depending on the period of the year. There are two time periods:

- Standard Time
- Daylight Saving Time - also referred to as summer time

If you want to know the time of a particular place in the United States, just use Google, indicating for example *time Dallas*.

CALLING TO THE BRANCH

A phone call to your bank branch is often not helpful.

First, your call is usually redirected to the bank's central office.

In addition, the bank clerk at the branch usually cannot help you with your Internet access or bank card problems.

Finally, you are often just a simple number. Do not rely on the bank clerk to remember your name.

BANK TELEPHONE NUMBERS

The bank offers you various ways to contact them by phone.

First, it offers a toll-free number, often referred to as a *numéro vert* in several European countries. However, this number is generally not available when a call is made from outside the United States.

In addition, there is never a single phone number to contact the bank. Often, there is a specific number for Internet access, another for bank cards, a third for small and medium-sized businesses, and so on. The multitude of phone numbers to contact the bank often creates a great deal of confusion for the customers.

Moreover, the waiting time before talking to a bank clerk is sometimes quite long. This is in addition to the fact that your call is often transferred from one department to another.

The rule is simple: stay patient while waiting.

INTERPRETER SERVICES

Did you know that major U.S. banks offer interpretation services in dozens of different languages? In less than five minutes, at your request, you can benefit from the services of an interpreter completely free of charge. It is just a matter of asking for it right from the start of your phone conversation with the bank clerk. For example, if you are French-speaking and uncomfortable in English, you simply have to say: *I need a French interpreter*.

IDENTIFICATION PROCEDURE

Next, the bank clerk must identify you. To do this, they will ask you a series of questions. Here are some of them:

- Your business or personal account number
- Your name
- The name of your company, if applicable
- Your address or that of your company
- Your telephone number or your company's number
- Your date of birth
- Your U.S. tax ID - SSN or ITIN - if it is a personal account
- The tax ID of your company - EIN - if it is a business account
- The address of the branch where the account was opened
- The date on which the account was opened
- The date and amount of your last deposit
- The date and amount of your last withdrawal
- The date and amount of your last payment by bank card

As for your name, remember that in the United States, your first name is followed by your last name. We do not introduce ourselves by saying Allard Vincent, but rather Vincent Allard.

In the case of an individual's U.S. tax ID - SSN or ITIN - if you do not have one, simply say so.

Never forget that the bank clerk already knows all the answers to the questions they ask you.

EFFECTIVENESS OF A PHONE CALL

A phone call to the bank's central number (not the branch) is one of the most effective and fastest ways to solve a problem related to your account, even if the waiting time is sometimes quite long before talking to a human being.

SUSPECTED PHONE CALL FROM THE BANK

If you receive a phone call from someone claiming to be an employee of your bank, tell yourself right away that this is a scam. Never reveal your personal information when you receive such a call. Instead, ask the person to send you an email with his or her request. However, never disclose your email address because the bank already has it on file.

2. EMAIL

The second way to contact the bank is by email. For this, you must use the messaging system offered inside your customer area. If you instead use a public email address of the bank, you will usually receive no response or, at most, a generic reply, due to the risk of identity fraud.

Your message must be written in English. If you have some difficulties in this language, online tools such as *Google Translate* or *DeepL* can help you.

Often, bank clerks misread your request and answer you anything. Their written answers are often prefabricated and not adapted to your specific needs.

Finally, beware of fake emails that claim to be sent on behalf of the bank. These are well-known scams and you should not add your name to the long list of victims.

∾

3. BRANCH

The third way to contact the bank is to physically visit one of its branches. It is absolutely not mandatory to go to the branch where your account was opened.

∾

4. WEBSITE

The fourth way to get information or help is to visit your bank's website. The FAQ section - for *Frequently Asked Questions* - usually contains a lot of information. In some cases, the help section will simply be called *Help*. Almost always, you will also find a link called *Customer Service*.

∾

5. SOCIAL NETWORKS

The fifth way to get information or help is to visit the bank's Facebook page. Some financial institutions will also use Twitter.

∾

6. APP ON YOUR MOBILE PHONE

The sixth way is to use the bank application you have in your mobile phone. Many banking applications offer in-app customer service through a chat feature. You may also schedule an appointment to meet a banker in person or by phone.

7. SEARCH ENGINE

Finally, the last way to get information about your account is to use a search engine, such as Google or Bing. Indeed, by using well-chosen keywords and indicating the name of your bank, you can find the information you are looking for in the blink of an eye, often faster than using the search tool on the bank's website.

4 - BUSINESS BANK ACCOUNT: FACTS AND SECRETS!

4.1 - CHOICE OF BANK

There are nearly 5,000 commercial banks in the United States. For customers, the choice is great. For banks, the competition is furious. Nevertheless, not all U.S. banks will accept to open an account for a foreigner, or for a U.S. company owned and managed by a foreigner. The common features of banks with which a foreigner can more easily open a business or personal account can be highlighted.

LARGE CITIES

First, banks located in large cities are more open to foreigners than those in smaller municipalities. For example, New York City, Miami, and Los Angeles are in daily contact with millions of foreigners. Bankers working in these three cities are used to meeting foreigners, hearing hundreds of different accents, and often even speaking their language.

BORDER CITIES

Second, banks located near U.S. borders, both in the north and south of the country, rely heavily on foreign customers to increase their revenues.

SMALL BANKS

Third, there are small local banks, constantly competing with major financial institutions. These small banks go out of their way to develop their clientele, and are often more open to outsiders who are serious.

U.S. SUBSIDIARIES OF FOREIGN BANKS

Fourth, U.S. subsidiaries of foreign banks are often favorably disposed to open an account for customers of their parent company.

OPENING A BANK ACCOUNT VIA THE INTERNET

Finally, several U.S. banks offer the option of opening an account online, without having to go to any branch. This seemingly interesting solution is often only offered to the following people:

- U.S. citizens
- U.S. residents
- People holding a U.S. Social Security Number - SSN
- People holding a U.S. non-resident tax ID - ITIN

Finally, here are three points you should remember.

1. BANKERS' REMUNERATION

Opening business accounts is a high-paying activity for American bankers. They are often paid on a commission basis. So, their desire to help you gives them a significant financial advantage.

2. BANK ACCOUNT IN THE UNITED STATES

In fact, there is no requirement for a U.S. company to open a bank account in the United States. However, it would be quite surprising, at least in the face of third parties, if a U.S. company did not have a bank account on U.S. soil.

3. COMPETITION

Every American bank is different. Each has its own set of rules. Each has its own compliance department, the size of which often varies with that of the bank itself. If a bank does not want to open an account for you or your company, another bank surely will. This is the beauty of the competition between banks.

4.2 - PREREQUISITES OF A BUSINESS ACCOUNT

Every U.S. bank has its own rules. Each bank also has its own requirements before agreeing to open a business account for your company.

Here is a non-exhaustive list of the prerequisites that a bank may have. However, this does not mean that it will require them all.

1. U.S. COMPANY

The first prerequisite concerns the nationality of your company. It has to be an American company. Therefore, it must have been created in one of the 50 states or the District of Columbia, where the capital city of the United States is located. It is almost impossible for a company created outside the United States to open a bank account on U.S. soil.

2. OFFICIAL DOCUMENTS

The second prerequisite concerns the official documents of your company. The bank will normally require a series of documents confirming the creation of your company and its current status. Often, these documents are in the corporate binder that you received following the creation of your company. A simple copy of these documents is often accepted by the banker.

Articles of Constitution

The first official document that the bank will normally require is a certified copy of your company's articles of constitution.

With respect to the corporation, its articles may have different names, depending on the state in which it was created. So we usually talk about:

- Articles of Incorporation
- Certificate of Incorporation
- Corporate Charter

With respect to the LLC, its articles may also bear different names, depending on the state in which it was created. So we usually talk about:

- Articles of Organization
- Certificate of Formation
- Certificate of Organization

Certificate of Good Standing

The second official document that the bank will normally require is a Certificate of Good Standing. This certificate is issued, upon your request, by the state in which your company was created. It confirms that your company exists and is in good standing with respect to the filing of its annual reports and the payment of the corporate tax.

Certificate of Incumbency

The third official document that the bank may require is a Certificate of Incumbency. It is a document that confirms the identity of the shareholders, as well as the identity of the directors and officers of your company, and their authority to open a bank account in its name. This document is normally signed by your company's organizer before a commissioner of oaths, known as a *notary public* in the United States.

Apostille

To add a character of authenticity to these three documents, they are sometimes supported by an apostille. It is a special seal applied by the state, which certifies that a document is a true copy of the original or that a document has been signed before a notary public. The apostille therefore adds a character of authenticity to the document, which is generally recognized almost everywhere in the world.

3. IDENTIFICATION DOCUMENTS

The third prerequisite is to confirm your identity. In this sense, the bank will usually ask you for at least two pieces of identification. If you are a foreigner, your passport is the most important one. Your driver's license or national identity card will also be required. In addition, as a foreigner, you will normally have to complete and sign the W-8BEN tax form - which can be found on irs.gov.

Note that the bank may sometimes discriminate against you, but without clearly disclosing it to you. This discrimination is based on several factors, including your citizenship, origin, or background.

For example, if you are a citizen of a country at war with the United States - military, political, commercial, or otherwise - you will not be welcome. If you come from a country on the U.S. government blacklist - for example, Iran, North Korea, or Cuba - do not even try to contact the bank. If you come from a country where the high rate of bank fraud is well known, the banker will not be able to help you.

If, despite this, you fall through the cracks of the banker's net, do not be surprised if the bank compliance department closes your account a few days or weeks later.

4. TAX ID – COMPANY

The fourth prerequisite concerns the tax ID of your American company. To open a business account in the United States, you must provide the bank with the tax ID of your company, which is its EIN. Without this number, it is absolutely impossible to open a business account. All you have to do is provide the banker with a copy of the Internal Revenue Service - IRS - letter confirming the EIN. If you have misplaced this letter, you can ask the IRS to fax you an EIN confirmation. This request is made by contacting the IRS by phone.

5. TAX ID – INDIVIDUAL

The fifth prerequisite is your own U.S. tax ID. Increasingly, banks are requiring you to provide them with your U.S. Social Security Number - SSN - or your U.S. Non-Resident Tax ID - ITIN. But you probably do not have any of these numbers. Some American banks will override this prerequisite, precisely by having you sign the W-8BEN form.

Another way to overcome this obstacle is to partner with a U.S. citizen, who will hold only a few shares in the capital stock of your company. This will often make it easier to open its bank account.

6. ADDRESS OF YOUR COMPANY

The sixth prerequisite concerns the address of your company. Most banks will require your company to have an address in the United States. In some cases, the bank will even send its representative to visit your establishment.

For example, your company was created in Delaware and uses an address in New York State. The New York banker will normally require you to provide New York's authorization for your Delaware corporation to do business there. Indeed, for New York State, any company that was not established there is considered a foreign company. However, if you do not have an establishment or employee in New York State, it is not necessarily a good idea to obtain the authorization required by the bank. As soon as you obtain this authorization from New York State, your company immediately enters the New York State tax system, which generally requires you to file a tax return and pay taxes in that state.

7. EMAIL ADDRESS

The seventh prerequisite is your email address. The bank will require the ability to communicate with you by email.

To give a serious image to your account opening process, it is recommended that your email address be as serious as you. Therefore, avoid providing the banker with:

- An email address like HeyYoMan@gmail.com
- An email address of a type notoriously used by hackers to encrypt their communications
- An email address with someone else's name

In any case, it is best to create a specific email address, which will include the name of your U.S. company. For example, for your company Best Business Inc., the email address can be BestBusiness@gmail.com or info@BestBusiness.com.

8. PHONE NUMBER

The eighth prerequisite is your phone. You will need to provide the bank with your phone number. In this sense, you should get a U.S. mobile phone. Alternatively, you can subscribe to a web service that will provide you with a virtual phone number, with call forwarding to your foreign phone.

In addition, there are websites that allow you to receive SMS or text messages virtually. However, these websites are not always as effective as a real U.S. mobile phone.

Finally, it is relatively easy to obtain an American or international SIM card online.

9. INITIAL DEPOSIT

The last prerequisite is the initial deposit. Generally, the minimum amount required is $100. However, the higher the initial deposit, the higher the banker's interest will be.

Avoid going to the bank with too much cash. It is not normal to bring $10,000 in cash to open a U.S. bank account. Above all, do not forget the obligations that the various laws impose on American banks, as we have seen previously.

Also, avoid bringing in foreign currency to open a bank account in the United States. American banks are often ill-equipped to receive foreign currency. Moreover, this may attract the attention of the banker, who is anxious to comply with all the obligations imposed by law.

An initial cash deposit, ranging from $100 to $1,000, is often the norm.

Finally, here are three points you should remember.

1. FOREIGN COMPANY

It is extremely rare, if not impossible, to open a bank account in the United States for your foreign company. It is therefore preferable to create an American subsidiary of your foreign company. Then, this subsidiary can take the appropriate steps to open its own U.S. bank account.

2. PHYSICAL PRESENCE

The bank normally requires your company to have a real physical presence in the United States. But in many cases, it will simply ask you the address of your company.

Many foreigners use a U.S. mailing address, or that of a relative, friend, or contact, to establish the domiciliation of their company and facilitate the opening of the business account.

3. DIFFERENT RULES

Remember that each U.S. bank has its own rules and requirements. Each bank, each district manager, each branch manager, and each banker often have their own rules. What is curious is that one branch of the bank will refuse to open a bank account, while another branch of the same bank will say yes. Go figure!

4.3 - SENSITIVE AREAS OF ACTIVITY

Generally, U.S. banks will open an account for most business activities a company can do.

However, there are at least five areas of activity that banks really do not like.

1. SEX

The first area of activity that embarrasses banks is the one reserved for adults. Therefore, any commercial activity related in any way to sex is rarely of interest to American banks.

Despite the fact that the United States is one of the largest producers of pornography in the world, banks are generally reluctant to open an account for everything related to this industry.

2. DRUGS

A second area of activity that is not of interest to banks is drugs. More states are legalizing the personal use of cannabis and other so-called soft drugs, such as Colorado. Despite this, banks do not dare open an account for companies working in this field.

3. FINANCIAL MANAGEMENT

A third area of activity that banks are rarely interested in is financial management for others. Banks want to be the only ones to manage money. Therefore, if your company provides financial management services for others, such as accepting cash deposits from its customers, banks will usually turn their backs on you.

However, do not confuse the financial management for others with the financial management of your own funds. Indeed, you may decide to create a U.S. company that will act as a holding company, for example to acquire interests in various companies or to make investments in certain projects. In this case, there is usually no problem to open a bank account for your personal management company.

4. GAMES AND LOTTERY

A fourth area of activity that does not attract banks is gambling and lotteries. Following a recent U.S. Supreme Court ruling, all 50 states now have the power to launch and manage gambling and lottery systems. Banks are cautious if such activities are offered by non-governmental companies. So, if you are planning to start a company that runs an online poker site, do not rely on a U.S. bank to open an account.

5. CRYPTOCURRENCIES

Finally, a fifth area of activity that does not interest banks is that of cryptocurrency. Although its development is booming, this payment tool is often identified with money laundering. As a result, particularly because of their obligations under various U.S. laws, banks are generally not interested in providing banking facilities to companies operating in this field.

Finally, here are three points you should remember.

1. IMAGE

U.S. banks are very conservative and image-conscious. In addition, they are subject to several regulatory agencies and hundreds of laws. Finally, the United States is deeply puritanical and conservative. In short, image is everything.

2. COMPETITION

There are nearly 5,000 commercial banks in the United States. Among these, there are some that are more open to foreigners than others. That is the beauty of the competition.

3. SOLUTION

There is always a solution to opening a bank account in the United States for your company. If some businesses are working in any of the five areas we have just covered, it means they have succeeded in opening a bank account. Contacts are therefore important in the banking world. The most difficult thing is opening your account. Then, you will see that things will go quite smoothly.

4.4 - AUTHORIZED SIGNATORIES

Who can be a signatory (signer) to a business bank account in the United States?

In the case of a corporation, its directors or officers generally have the authority to act as signatories on the bank account.

In the case of an LLC, its managers usually have the same authority.

SIGNATORIES TO AVOID

However, it is best not to appoint someone who is not a director or officer of your company as a signatory, to minimize the risk of fraud.

The same applies to a minority shareholder, who does not have the same financial interests as the majority shareholder of your company.

Finally, it is recommended that you never use the services of a nominee director to act as a signatory on your company's bank account. American banks want to do business with the real representatives of your company.

NUMBER OF SIGNATORIES

It is best to appoint two signatories on the bank account, unless you are the sole director and officer of your company.

Ideally, there should be no more than two authorized signatories. Otherwise, it often becomes difficult to manage the situation, especially when there are frequent departures or replacements of directors or officers.

SIGNATURES REQUIRED ON CHECKS

If you would like each check issued by your company to require two signatures, note that banks do not routinely verify this.

Banks no longer want to assume responsibility for managing the number of signatures required on a check. In other words, all your checks will usually be honored by your bank, regardless of whether they have one or two signatures.

Of course, the large amount of a check can sometimes attract the attention of the bank, which will verify it before clearing it.

CHANGE, ADDITION, OR WITHDRAWAL OF SIGNATORIES

In case of change, addition, or withdrawal of authorized signatories to the bank account, a new signature card is invariably required by the bank.

This means that all authorized signatories, both existing and new, must sign a new signature card. This also implies that all signatories must present themselves at the same time to the bank for this purpose.

It is also necessary to cancel any bank card and Internet access granted to former signatories.

DEATH OF A SIGNATORY

Finally, upon your death, this can be a problem if you are the only signatory. For some time after your death, no one will be able to access the company's bank account. In such a situation, it will be preferable for your estate to immediately refer the case to a U.S. lawyer in order to resolve the situation quickly.

The precaution of appointing two authorized signatories therefore becomes crucial, especially when one of the signatories dies. In such a case, the company can still continue its banking operations without problem and replace the deceased signatory in the normal course of business.

4.5 - USE OF THE BANK ACCOUNT

The use of a U.S. bank account is not a right. It is a privilege granted by the bank to both American citizens and foreigners. The contractual relationship with the bank, confirmed in writing, is not negotiable. Like you, the bank can terminate the contract at any time, without disclosing the reason for its decision.

NORMAL USE

It is therefore recommended to use your bank account in a normal way. The usual activity of an account includes deposits, withdrawals, and payments by bank card, all on a regular basis. If you use your account as a simple container - for example, to receive transfers from abroad, which immediately go abroad - be assured that the bank compliance department will close your account without notice.

CASH

In addition, you should avoid depositing cash into your account unless your company is in an industry that generates this type of income. For example, a restaurant or hair salon will regularly deposit cash into its account.

You should also avoid withdrawing cash from an ATM or at the bank if it comes from your business account.

In general, a U.S. company withdraws money in three ways:

- By check
- By transfer
- By payment with bank card

If you withdraw cash on a regular basis, you could draw the attention of the bank compliance department.

LARGE DEPOSITS AND WITHDRAWALS

Also, it may be helpful to notify your bank if you are about to make an important transaction or receive a significant deposit into your account. The recommendation is the same if you plan to make a significant withdrawal. In other words, keep your banker informed.

TAXATION

Finally, simply having a bank account in the United States can have legal and tax consequences for you or your company. As a result, you may need to complete and file forms in the United States, in your country of residence, or both. In this regard, it is recommended to consult a U.S. tax specialist working in your jurisdiction.

4.6 - ONE BANK ACCOUNT IS OK. BUT...

In these uncertain times, it is increasingly difficult to put all your trust in a single bank.

REASONS

Many believe that:

- The global financial crisis, which began in 2007, was largely caused by U.S. banks.
- Banks' priorities are strictly limited to the financial performance for their shareholders and the overwhelmingly comfortable well-being of their executives and senior managers.
- The bank customer is a simple account number to which fewer and fewer services are offered for an ever higher price.
- Some banks sometimes commit reprehensible acts, often sanctioned by significant government fines.

REALITY

Since the tragic day of September 11, 2001, U.S. banks are no longer run by bankers (normally in contact with customers), but by their compliance departments (having no contact with customers).

How many times have I seen such a compliance department close a bank account, without any notice, without having contacted the customer, and without the banker at the branch being informed or being able to do anything about it.

NO EXPLANATION

No reason for closing the account is usually provided to the customer. When a U.S. bank opens your account, it gives you contractual notice that it can close your account at any time, upon written notice and without having to provide you with any reason. Above all, do not confuse *Notice* with *Prior Notice*. When you receive the notice from the bank, your account is usually already closed.

LIST OF REASONS

Here is a non-exhaustive list of the reasons why the bank may close your account:

- You do not live on American soil.
- You do not have a U.S. social security number — SSN.
- You do not have an individual taxpayer identification number — ITIN.
- Your account shows suspicious fund movements.
- A transfer received from abroad seems suspicious.
- Your account has a positive balance that is too low.
- Your account has a negative balance.
- Your account remains inactive for more than six months.

CONSEQUENCES

After the account is closed, the bank will issue a check to your company - regardless of the size of the balance - and send it to you by regular mail, sometimes by special delivery. But what to do with this check if your company no longer has a bank account to cash it?

SOLUTION

The solution is simple: always deal with two banks, that is to say, have a bank account in each of them. You are under no obligation to grant exclusivity of your financial activities to a single bank, except on rare occasions. The main principle in business is to divide and conquer.

In addition, do not disclose to Bank no. 1 your relationship with Bank no. 2 - and vice versa - unless required in a specific bank contract. So, let each banker believe that he or she is unique in the world.

ADVANTAGES

There are many advantages of having a bank account in two different banks:

- This allows you to build a business relationship with two banks on a parallel basis.
- This allows you to compare the nature, quality, and price of services.
- This allows you to enjoy the best of each bank.
- This saves you from being at the mercy of a single bank if your account is closed abruptly.
- This prevents a single bank from knowing all of your financial assets or those of your company.
- This allows you to take advantage of the $250,000 FDIC guarantee for each of your bank accounts.

DISADVANTAGES

The disadvantages are rather rare:

- First, this leads to a double bank reconciliation every month.
- Second, this may result in additional bank charges - although it is relatively easy to find a bank account at no cost in the United States.

REAL-LIFE CASE

Since its founding in 2001, CorpoMax has been dealing with two banks. Each of CorpoMax's bank accounts has a specific mission:

- Account no. 1: Current transactions
- Account no. 2: Receipt of bank transfers

Having two bank accounts has always been very useful for CorpoMax. For example:

- In 2011, during the acquisition of its own commercial building, CorpoMax involved the two banks to finance the acquisition cost - Bank no. 1 - and the renovation work - Bank no. 2.
- If CorpoMax deposits a foreign check issued in foreign currency — for example, a Canadian dollar check drawn on a Canadian bank —Bank no. 1 charges a fee of $75 per check, not to mention a clearing period of 30 to 60 days. However, if CorpoMax deposits the same check at Bank no. 2, the fee is only $5 and the clearing occurs 24 to 48 hours later.

ACCOUNTS IN THE SAME BANK

It is also possible to have two accounts within the same bank. For example, your company has two different divisions or websites. In such a case, one bank account per division or per website can facilitate your accounting operations. It is quite common in the United States for a company to have more than one account with the same bank.

ACCOUNTS IN A FOREIGN COUNTRY

It also happens that some companies open a bank account outside the United States, in addition to their U.S. account. This can be explained if some of their activities are carried out abroad. Another reason may be that their activities take place mainly in a foreign currency. This avoids currency conversion costs.

As mentioned earlier, there is no obligation for a company to open a bank account in the United States. However, it would be quite surprising if a U.S. company did not have a bank account on American soil, at least in the eyes of its U.S. customers and suppliers.

4.7 - NEED A REAL CREDIT CARD?

If you are not a U.S. citizen or tax resident, it is almost impossible for you to obtain a credit card in the United States. Here, we are not talking about an ATM card or a debit card. We are talking about a credit card, allowing you to make purchases but pay later, usually on a monthly basis.

However, here are some solutions.

DESERVE

For example, the Deserve.com website allows foreign students and holders of certain types of U.S. visas to obtain a credit card. What is interesting is that these cardholders do not need to have a U.S. Social Security Number - SSN - or a credit history in the United States.

SECURED CARDS

In addition, some major U.S. banks offer secured cards. Generally, this type of card is granted to a person, not a business. The bank asks you to place a minimum amount in a bank account, to cover at least the credit limit granted on the card. This amount is frozen as long as you hold the secured credit card. To obtain this type of card, you must normally go to one of the bank's branches. Finally, a secured card usually has an annual fee.

INTERNATIONAL BANK CARDS

Some websites also offer the possibility of obtaining an international bank card, often combined with a bank-type account. For example, TransferWise, Payoneer, Netspend, and Payza offer solutions to consider.

PARENT OR FRIEND IN THE UNITED STATES

Finally, if you have a relative or friend who resides in the United States and agrees to help you, they can normally add you as an authorized user on their own credit card account. Indeed, with their U.S. Social Security Number, they can, without much difficulty, add a second cardholder.

Finally, here are three points you should remember.

1. ITIN

The ITIN tax identifier typically allows non-U.S. residents to build a credit history in the United States with leading credit bureaus Equifax, Trans-Union, and Experian.

2. ADDRESS IN THE UNITED STATES

To obtain a U.S. credit card, it is essential to have an address on American soil. If you do not own a property in the United States, an address can be obtained in a variety of ways, including through a domiciliation service, a parent, or a friend.

3. IDENTIFICATION

If you do not have a U.S. Social Security Number - SSN - or a U.S. Non-Resident Tax ID - ITIN - some banks will accept an international identification such as your passport. If you are not physically present at the branch, these banks will often require that a copy of your ID be authenticated by a U.S embassy or consulate.

4.8 - BANK COMPLIANCE DEPARTMENT

Since September 11, 2001, as we have seen previously, several U.S. laws have been adopted, notably the *USA Patriot Act*. These laws impose several obligations on American banks, including having a compliance department.

ROLE OF THE COMPLIANCE DEPARTMENT

The role of the compliance department is to verify everything, from opening to closing bank accounts, not to mention the use of the funds that pass through them. The larger the bank in terms of assets and active accounts, the more important the compliance department is. The rumor is that, in the compliance department of major American banks, several FBI agents - U.S. Federal Police - work there full-time. Their role is to verify the nature of transactions, the source of funds, and their use. In addition, the compliance department regularly conducts audits in branches.

CRITICAL PERIOD

When you are a foreigner, it is difficult to open a bank account in the United States. The most critical period lasts 90 days after opening this account. Indeed, it is often during this three-month period that the compliance department reviews the parameters for opening the bank account and analyses the movement of funds, both in and out. At the end of this period, there is generally no problem. But never forget that your business or personal account must always be managed and used in a normal way.

Finally, here are three points you should remember.

1. OPEN AND CLOSED

Today, a U.S. bank account is opened by the banker and potentially closed by the compliance department.

2. PRIOR NOTICE

Often, the compliance department does not give any notice to the customer or banker before closing an account. Instead, a written notice from the bank is sent when the account is closed, followed by a check for the amount of the remaining balance.

3. REASONS FOR CLOSURE

The compliance department does not reveal the cause of the bank account's closure to either the customer or the banker. Under the contract with the customer, the bank has no need to disclose the reasons for closing the account.

4.9 - CLOSING THE BANK ACCOUNT

There are three types of bank account closure.

1. AUTOMATIC CLOSURE

The first type of closure is without human intervention.

The first case of automatic closure occurs when your account becomes overdrawn. If you do not quickly fill the overdraft, the bank's automated system will close your account without notice. However, some banks are slightly tolerant of the authorized overdraft, subject to significant bank fees. If your account is closed due to an overdraft, it is rare for the bank to agree to reopen your account, even if you fill the overdraft shortly thereafter. In such a case, after your payment, it may agree to open a new account.

The second case of automatic closure occurs when your account is inactive for a specified period of time. For example, you do not make any transactions for six months. In such a case, the bank will contact you in writing so that you can reactivate your account within 30 days. Generally, reactivation is done simply by making a deposit or withdrawal. If you do not reactivate, your bank account is automatically closed. Funds that are dormant in your account are then generally remitted to the state in which the original bank branch is located. In some cases, banks agree to reopen a closed account due to inactivity.

2. CLOSURE BY THE BANKER

The second type of closure is by the banker.

The first case of account closure by the banker occurs when your company makes a name change. Indeed, U.S. banks will usually close your company's bank account and open a new one, this time with your company's new name. However, some banks simply agree to change the name of your company on the existing account.

The second case of account closure by the banker occurs when you ask them to close your account. However, it is recommended that you cash all checks made payable to your company before closing the account completely. This may seem obvious, but sometimes busy entrepreneurs close their company's bank account and then receive a check from the IRS as a tax refund. It then becomes difficult, if not impossible, to cash a check when the company, now dissolved, no longer has a bank account in the United States.

3. CLOSURE BY THE COMPLIANCE DEPARTMENT

The third type of closure is by the compliance department.

Here are some examples of situations that cause such a closure:

- Constant access to your bank account via the Internet from abroad
- Frequent cash withdrawals, at the teller or through the ATM — mostly from a business bank account
- Frequent cash deposits, unless this is common in your industry — for example, catering or hairdressing

- Deceit by using non-existent funds (check kiting)

Be aware, this list is not exhaustive.

4.10 - PERSONAL BANK ACCOUNT: SOME TIPS

When doing business in the United States, it may be useful to not only have a business bank account, but also a personal one. Indeed, it may be convenient to have such an account, especially if your company has to reimburse you for expenses, or pay you a salary or dividends.

EASIER

In general, if you are a non-resident of the United States, it is easier to open a personal account than a business one. This is the case in most major American cities, such as New York and Miami. These cities are accustomed to welcoming millions of visitors every year. This is also the case for banks located near U.S. borders.

PREREQUISITES

When you go to the bank, the bankers normally require you to present them with two pieces of identification, including your passport. They also ask you to provide them with a U.S. address and a U.S. telephone number. As we have seen previously, it is relatively easy to subscribe

to a domiciliation service and to obtain a telephone number in the
United States.

SAME BANK

In an ideal world, your personal account will be located at the same
bank as your business account. This will make it much easier to make
transfers from one account to the other, usually at no charge.

4.11 - ALTERNATIVE SOLUTIONS

More alternative solutions are available to those who want to open a business or personal bank account in the United States.

ONLINE "BANKS"

Indeed, a series of new players in the financial field regularly appear on the Internet. These sites offer several services previously exclusive to banks, including the following:

- Multi-currency business accounts
- Multi-currency personal accounts
- International debit cards, with Visa or MasterCard logo
- Transfers between your accounts
- Transfers to other accounts

You will find a partial list of these sites in the *Useful Resources* section.

MONEY TRANSFERS

In addition, web solutions offering the possibility of making money transfers at a reasonable price are multiplying.

Again, you will find many of these sites in the *Useful Resources* section.

STOCK TRADING SITES

Finally, some websites offer facilities that may resemble those of a traditional bank account. These include sites that allow individuals to conduct stock market transactions online. For non-U.S. residents, the application for an account cannot be made online. However, it is sometimes possible to achieve your goals by contacting the customer service at these websites.

Increasingly, U.S. banks are feeling the heat, precisely because of these newcomers. And it is only the beginning.

5 - MERCHANT ACCOUNT AND PAYPAL: YES, IT IS POSSIBLE!

5.1 - MERCHANT ACCOUNT - VISA, MASTERCARD, AMEX, DISCOVER

In the United States, the financial tool most used by consumers is the credit card.

POPULAR CARDS

The most popular card is Visa, which has 323 million cardholders. In second place is the MasterCard, with 191 million cardholders. In third place, on equal footing, are Discover and American Express cards, each with approximately 58 million cardholders.

FIRST CARD NUMBER

For your information, the credit card numbers always start with:

- 3 for American Express
- 4 for Visa
- 5 for MasterCard
- 6 for Discover

CARDS ON YOUR MOBILE PHONE

More U.S. consumers are using their mobile phones to make card payments. For now, the main actors are:

- Apple Pay
- Google Pay
- Samsung Pay

MERCHANT ACCOUNT

If you want your company to offer payment facilities to its customers, you must obtain a merchant account.

A merchant account is a type of bank account that allows businesses to accept payments made using credit or debit cards. This account is established under an agreement between a merchant - your company - and a bank or aggregator - intermediary - for the settlement of payment card transactions.

MERCHANT ACCOUNT PROVIDERS

There are various types of merchant account providers in the United States.

Banks

First of all, U.S. banks usually offer this service. They allow your company to accept payments made by Visa, MasterCard, Discover, and now American Express - which used to operate independently. Being conservative, banks do not take unnecessary risks. This means that it is particularly difficult to obtain a merchant account from them, especially if you are a foreigner or if your company does not have an establishment in the United States. In addition, the commission rates charged by banks are generally quite high.

General Providers

Second, there are the general providers of merchant accounts. In the United States, there are more than 2,500 general providers. Competition is therefore important, which is beneficial for companies that want to offer payment facilities to their customers.

A list of the most popular merchant account providers in the United States can be found in the *Useful Resources* section.

Specialized Providers — High Risk

Third, there are providers specialized in high risk. High-risk business sectors are those whose credit card transactions result in a significant amount of chargebacks. These sectors include the following:

- Dating sites
- Downloadable software
- Fortune tellers
- Games and betting
- Websites for adults only

As a result, these specialized providers generally require a higher commission rate. In addition, a security deposit is sometimes required. Finally, payments to their customers are also more distant in time than those of general providers. For example, if a transaction occurs on May 1st, you will receive your payment maybe two or three weeks later.

You will find a list of some specialized suppliers in the *Useful Resources* section.

MERCHANT ACCOUNT BROKERS

It is not always easy to navigate the sea of merchant account providers in the United States. Fortunately, there are brokers who specialize in obtaining a merchant account. These brokers are in constant contact with several merchant account providers. This allows them to be familiar with each other's strengths and weaknesses and to offer their customers sound advice.

A list of these rare brokers can be found in the *Useful Resources* section.

5.2 - PAYPAL ACCOUNT

PayPal is a major player in the financial sector in the United States. This company is one of the leading merchant account providers in the country. But there is also the traditional PayPal, which is widely used all over the world.

RECOMMENDATIONS

When you create your U.S. company, you should normally open a PayPal account for it immediately.

Here are two important recommendations:

- First, go to paypal.com to create a new account for your company, not the PayPal website in your country of residence - for example, paypal.fr.
- Second, do not use the email address linked to your personal PayPal account to create your company's account. It is better to create a brand new email address, specific to your company, and use it to open its PayPal account.

IF YOU ARE A FOREIGNER

It is not always easy to open a U.S. PayPal account for your American company, especially when you are a foreigner. However, there are a number of ways to do this, including contacting PayPal customer service by phone. When your company's PayPal account is set up, you can ask PayPal, again by phone, to have the amounts received in your account deposited daily into your company's business bank account.

ADVANTAGES

The huge advantage of PayPal is that it is very popular with consumers. It is easy to pay with PayPal. Another important advantage is the security of transactions. Consumers do not need to disclose their credit card number to the merchant during the purchase transaction, which is reassuring.

DISADVANTAGES

However, there are some disadvantages. First, the commission rate charged by PayPal is generally higher than that of traditional merchant account providers. Second, PayPal sometimes decides - without notice - to freeze funds in your PayPal account, up to six months. The reasons given by PayPal vary according to circumstances and are allegedly based on risk factors. This is why it is strongly recommended to set up the automatic money transfer procedure from your PayPal account to your company's bank account on a daily basis.

6 - CONCLUSION

6.1 - IF I WERE YOU...

If I were you, that is, if I were:

- A foreigner, without a U.S. tax identifier — SSN or ITIN
- Who does not live in the United States
- Who wants to open a bank account for his or her company,

here is what I would do.

1. CREATE A U.S. COMPANY

First of all, if I were you, I would create a U.S. company. On the one hand, it is virtually impossible to open a business bank account for a foreign company in the United States. On the other hand, Americans buy first and foremost American. If you are targeting the U.S. market, you need to give your company an American identity, which will immediately attract more American consumers.

The logic of an American corporate identity is easy to remember:

- U.S. company
- U.S. address
- U.S. phone number
- U.S. bank account

By creating your company in the United States, this will give you a significant competitive advantage.

2. COME TO THE UNITED STATES

Second, if I were you, I would come to the United States. It is much easier to successfully open a bank account when you are physically in front of the banker. Remember there are almost 5,000 U.S. commercial banks, which are in constant competition with each other. If a first bank does not want to open an account for your company, the second probably will. If it also refuses because you do not reside in the United States, a third bank may have lower requirements.

But do not come to the United States to open a bank account. Instead, come here on vacation and take the opportunity to visit banks. For example, you will never forget your vacation in New York, a city that never sleeps.

Are you uncomfortable speaking English? Do not worry. First, there are banks where some employees speak more than one language. Second, banks located in major cities are used to meeting foreigners who speak hundreds of different languages. Finally, there are mobile applications that instantly translate your words into the language of your choice.

3. GET A U.S. MOBILE PHONE

Third, if I were you, I would buy a U.S. mobile phone. This provides at least two benefits. First, the phone can receive SMS or text messages that can be sent from time to time by the bank, for security purposes. Second, if you use a U.S. address when you buy your mobile phone, this is, for some banks at least, proof of address in the United States. Another solution, often cheaper, is to get a U.S. or international SIM card.

4. OPEN A BUSINESS AND PERSONAL BANK ACCOUNT

Fourth, if I were you, I would open not only a business bank account for my U.S. company, but also a personal account. The advantage of holding these two accounts is the ease of transferring money from one account to the other. For example, if your company has to reimburse you for expenses or pay you a dividend or salary, nothing is easier than transferring money from your business account to your personal one.

In addition, remember that bankers' pay in the United States is often based on the number of accounts they open. These bankers therefore have every interest in opening a maximum number of bank accounts. That is why month-ends are often a good time to open a bank account in the United States: bankers absolutely want to reach their monthly performance goals.

Also, if I were you, I would open each of these accounts in two different banks. Indeed, you should never be at the mercy of a single bank, whose compliance department may decide to close any of your accounts without notice or reason.

5. GET AN ITIN

Finally, if I were you, I would apply for an ITIN identifier. Although of a tax nature, this equivalent of the SSN for non-U.S. residents - is widely used in the United States by various financial actors to identify you: banks, merchant account providers, PayPal, etc. Some banks accept only the SSN, but several also accept the ITIN as an equivalent.

A U.S. Certified Public Accountant - CPA - or a U.S. tax specialist will usually be able to assist you in obtaining an ITIN.

FINAL WORD

You now have two important assets:

- The knowledge of the U.S. banking system and its components
- The tools to open a business and personal bank account in the United States.

The life of an entrepreneur is often full of pitfalls, obstacles, and annoyances. This should not discourage you at all. This is part of the life of an entrepreneur.

If you really want to, you will be able to open a business bank account for your U.S. company, as well as a personal account for your own needs.

If you enjoyed this practical guide, feel free to post a comment on the website where you got it.

If you have any questions, comments, or suggestions, please do not hesitate to contact me.

Thank you and good luck in your American adventure!

USEFUL RESOURCES

You will find the list of useful resources at:

www.corpomax.com/open

This list of useful resources is constantly updated and enriched, especially by your contributions.

If you find a site or a web page that should be in this list, please do not hesitate to send me the link.

In addition, if any of the links on this list are broken, please let me know.

Happy surfing!

ACKNOWLEDGMENTS

I would like to sincerely thank:

- My wife **Sylvie DUSSAULT ALLARD**, Director of Customer Service at CorpoMax, who always shares my creative and literary impulses - often in spite of herself
- My son **Jérémie ALLARD**, who meticulously revised the English version of the three practical guides, in addition to being the narrator in their audio version
- My stepdaughter **Véronique ALLARD**, Managing Director at CorpoMax, with whom I have had the pleasure of working for more than 10 years
- My friend **Marie-Andrée LEMIEUX**, highly talented artist, who has been taking care of my imaging and graphic design needs since 1995
- My colleague **Bettina KARPEL**, lawyer and legal translator, who has been working on my translation needs since 1995
- My friend **Christine BUREAU**, virtual collaborator and responsible for the launch of the practical guides in the *Yes to Entrepreneurs*® series

ABOUT VINCENT ALLARD

Since 1981, Vincent Allard has been a lawyer and a member of the Quebec Bar. He is also a member of the Canadian Bar Association and the American Bar Association.

He holds three university degrees:

- Law degree - LL.L. - from University of Montréal
- Master of Business Law - LL.M. - University of Ottawa, Canada
- Master of Business Administration - MBA - from École des HEC in Montreal, Canada.

For 18 years, Vincent Allard practiced business law, including corporate law and commercial litigation, primarily as a founding partner of the Pigeon, Allard law firm in Montreal.

In 1995, he co-founded Jurifax (jurifax.com), a legal publishing company that distributes more than 600 legal forms and other legal products via the Internet.

In 2001, shortly after emigrating to the United States, he founded CorpoMax (corpomax.com). Located in the state of Delaware, CorpoMax offers U.S. company formation and U.S. trademark services to thousands of entrepreneurs and professionals working in more than 50 countries.

In 2017, he launched DictoMax (dictomax.com), which offers online training to entrepreneurs and professionals.

In 2020, Vincent Allard published three practical guides for entrepreneurs:

- In English and French
- In digital, paperback, and audio formats
- All part of the *Yes to Entrepreneurs*® series.

For more than 15 years, Vincent Allard has provided training on the organization and launch of companies in the United States, mainly to foreign entrepreneurs, lawyers, accountants and tax specialists.

TO CONTACT VINCENT ALLARD

- Email: vallard@corpomax.com
- Phone: +1 302 266 8200
- Skype: corpomax

linkedin.com/in/corpomax

twitter.com/corpomax

youtube.com/corpomax

facebook.com/corpomax

BOOKS BY VINCENT ALLARD

www.corpomax.com/practical-guides

❧

How to Start Your Business in the United States

Create Your U.S. Company

in Delaware or Elsewhere in the USA

How to Name Your Business in the United States

Find and Protect the Name of Your Company

in the United States and Abroad

How to Open Your Bank Account in the United States

Open and Manage Your

Business or Personal Account in the USA

❧

Ces livres sont aussi disponibles en français :

www.corpomax.com/guides-pratiques

LEGAL INFORMATION

Every effort has been made to make this guide as complete and accurate as possible. Although the author and the publisher have prepared this guide with the greatest of care, and have made every effort to ensure the accuracy, they assume no responsibility or liability for errors, inaccuracies, or omissions. Before you begin, check with the appropriate authorities to ensure compliance with all laws and regulations.

On the other hand, this guide may contain mistakes in typography or content. Also, this guide contains information valid only until the date of its publication.

Therefore, this practical guide should be used as a guide only - not as the ultimate source of information. The purpose of this guide is for educational purposes only. The author and the publisher do not warrant that the information contained in this guide is fully complete and shall not be responsible for any errors or omissions. The author and the publisher shall have neither liability nor responsibility to any person or entity with respect to any loss or damage caused or alleged to be caused directly or indirectly by this guide, nor do they make any claims or promises of your ability to generate income by using any of the information contained in this guide.

Finally, the list of useful resources, which is offered as a bonus with this guide, contains a series of hyperlinks, which are provided for informational purposes only. The author and the publisher do not guarantee that the information contained in the websites concerned by these hyperlinks is complete, adequate or truthful. Therefore, the author and the publisher incur no liability to any person or entity for any loss or damage caused or suspected to be caused directly or indirectly by the use of the information contained in one or more of the websites concerned. The author and publisher make no representation or promise of your ability to generate income by using the information contained in one or more of the relevant websites.

Made in the USA
Middletown, DE
20 May 2021

40134835R00086